W9-AOM-847

SERVICE
LEARNING

Volunteering to Help the Environment

Suzanne J. Murdico

HIGH
interest
books

Children's Press
A Division of Grolier Publishing
New York / London / Hong Kong / Sydney
Danbury, Connecticut

For my niece and goddaughter, Amy Lynn Kowell

Photo Credits: Cover, © FPG Internationa; p. 4 Thaddeus Harden; p. 6, 27, 28 © Uniphoto; p. 8 © Daemmrich/Uniphoto; p. 12 © Joseph Sohm/Uniphoto; p.15 © Ralph A. Clevenger/Corbis; p. 16, 18 © Joseph Sohm/Corbis; p. 20 © Todd Gipstein/Corbis; p. 23 © David H. Wells/Corbis; p. 24, 39 © Indexstock; p. 31 © Frank Siteman/Uniphoto; p. 32, 34, 36, 40 David Skjold

Contributing Editor: Mark Beyer
Book Design: Michael DeLisio

Visit Children's Press on the Internet at:
http://publishing.grolier.com

Cataloging-in-Publication Data

Murdico, Suzanne J.
    Volunteering to help the environment / Suzanne J. Murdico.
    p. cm. – (Service learning)
    ISBN 0-516-23373-4 (lib. bdg.)– ISBN 0-516-23573-7 (pbk.)
    1. Environmental protection – Citizen participation – Juvenile literature
    2. Student service – Juvenile literature   3. Volunteer workers in environmental protection – Juvenile literature   4. Voluntarism – Juvenile literature I. Title II. Series
    TD171.7.M867   2000
    363.7'0525—dc21

CONTENTS

INTRODUCTION

Volunteering to help people and the environment is not new. People have been helping others for hundreds of years. Today's service-learning programs combine volunteering and learning. By volunteering to help people and the community, volunteers learn skills that will help them throughout their lives. These skills include how to plan a project, how best to work with others, and how to share their experience with others.

Sometimes volunteering can earn you credit toward graduation. Sometimes, volunteering is required to graduate. In either case, if you volunteer, children do not go hungry, seniors feel less alone, and the environment is cleaner and safer.

Volunteering to help the environment is important to us all. Today, we know that environmental problems will not go away by

Volunteering helps you meet new people while you help others in need.

themselves. We need to start using water, oil, natural gas, and coal wisely. These are our natural resources. Some natural resources can't be replaced once they have been used up. They are called nonrenewable resources. We need to take care of our environment. Cleanup campaigns, recycling, and conservation efforts are helping to improve the environment. Volunteers like you can help make a difference. You can start helping right in your own community!

Environmental cleanup projects are a great way to begin volunteering.

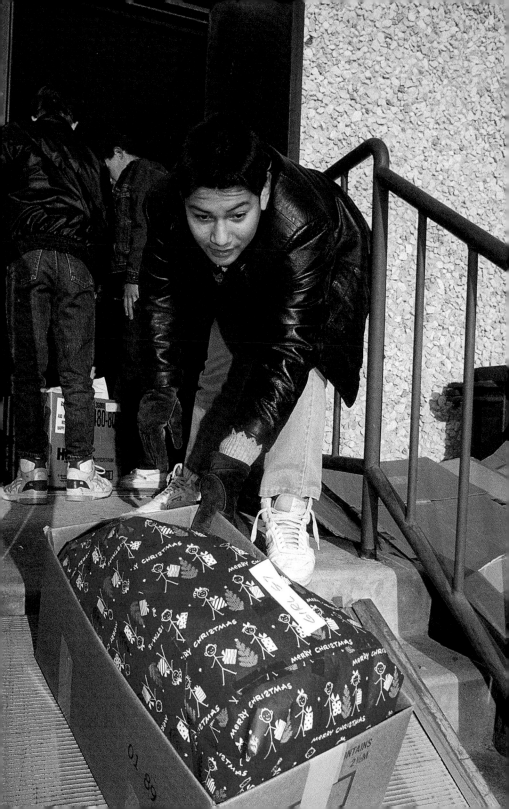

CHAPTER ONE

WHAT IS SERVICE LEARNING?

SERVICE LEARNING VS. COMMUNITY SERVICE

Both service learning and community service use volunteer (unpaid) workers in the community. However, service-learning project leaders understand that it is not enough just to have a volunteer's time and effort. These leaders want volunteers to learn about the project and themselves. They want volunteers to help plan a project and learn a skill, such as how to write a letter to a public official. They want volunteers to understand how their efforts help people and the community. Understanding each of these empowers volunteers to do things on their own.

Helping to give needy children gifts teaches students that communities can work together.

HELPING PEOPLE AND THE COMMUNITY

As a volunteer, you donate your time, energy, and skills to a project. If you volunteer to help the community, you help to make your community a better place in which to live. There are many ways in which you can help. You can help people by reading to blind seniors, working at a shelter to feed the homeless, or teaching younger kids to play a sport. You can help the environment by picking up litter around your school, writing letters to public officials about pollution in your town or city, or holding a glass or plastic recycling drive. These projects are simple to develop and easy to run. All they take is your involvement. What's more, being involved has a great benefit to your future.

BENEFITS TO THE VOLUNTEER

If you know how to organize people to help on a project, you have gained management skills. If you can talk with people and write an effective letter to officials, you have gained communication skills. If you complete a success-ful project, you have shown others (and yourself) that you have what it takes to stay with a project until it is finished. Each of these skills has helped you to succeed on this pro-ject. And, all of these skills can be listed on a college application form. They show college admissions officials that a student can be a success.

DID YOU KNOW?

According to the National Service-Learning Clear-inghouse, nearly 3 million high school students are involved in service-learn-ing projects every year. For middle school students, that number is 2.5 million.

Beyond college is the workplace. When you are ready to get a job, you must prepare a document of your education, past jobs, vol-unteer projects, and awards you may have earned. This is called a resumé. List on your

Neighborhood cleanups are the first step toward making a neighborhood safe for everyone.

resumé the volunteer projects you have completed. This will show potential employers that you have the skills to help their business.

BENEFITS TO THE COMMUNITY

By volunteering in your community, you'll improve your own neighborhood. For example, a local playground may be overgrown with weeds. Are the steel basketball hoops bent? Is the swing set rusted? Is the ground beneath the children's play sets dirt? Is the fence around the playground torn and dangerous?

You could help to clean up this playground. You can help pull the weeds and cut the grass. You can help take down the basketball hoops and buy new ones with money raised or donated. You can paint the swing set. You can lay wood chips over the dirt so rain doesn't make the playground muddy. You can repair the fence or help put up a new fence. You'll be helping people you know. This includes your neighbors and friends. Your efforts will make this playground a safe and inviting place for neighborhood teens and children. Working together with other volunteers helps to build community spirit and pride.

HELPING THE ENVIRONMENT

Volunteering is connected to people, the community, and the environment. And, everything is connected in the environment. We breathe the air, drink the water, and live on the land. However, factories also use the air, water, and land. Without factories, we would not have homes, books, televisions, or furniture. But, factories can pollute the environment.

Pollution doesn't only come from factories. People litter by throwing bottles, cans, plastic, batteries, paper, and even food on the ground instead of in trash cans. We all live in areas that suffer from some kind of pollution.

The air, water, and land that we live near and use must be made to last. Sometimes, to make the environment last, we must all pitch in and help. You can help the environment by picking up trash and recycling metal, plastic, and paper. Do you know if your school has recycling programs? Think of all the paper, bottles, and cans that a school uses. You can get involved in an effort to have your school start recycling.

There are many examples of programs that you can join to help the environment. You can get involved in a battery-recycling program, hold an environmental fair at your

Pollution coming from factories is something against which volunteers can fight.

Roadway improvement includes tree planting projects.

school, or join a group that plants trees around your neighborhood. You can be on a team that repairs a sidewalk, cleans a stream, or paints over graffiti. Does your playground need a drinking fountain? Is there an abandoned building in your neighborhood? Does your drinking water contain lead or chemicals? You can encourage community groups and businesses to use recycled products. You can start an environmental club. You can hold a recycling contest. There are many ways to help your environment. You just have to know how to get involved.

CHAPTER TWO

GETTING STARTED

So, you want to get involved in a service-learning project that helps the environment. First, you'll need to find a group that is sponsoring an activity. Second, you'll need to find a worthwhile project for which you'll volunteer your time. Finally, you'll want to make sure that you're the best volunteer you can be.

SCHOOL-BASED SPONSORS

The first place to look for a project sponsor is at your school. In 1990, President George Bush signed into law the National Community Service Act. This law set aside nearly $62 million for schools to use in developing service-learning projects. Each year, more money is put into the program. Students are encouraged to join a school-sponsored volunteer group. Schools advertise for volunteers in student newspapers or bulletins, and in individual classes. Teachers lead the volunteer groups. You can find out more about the individual projects offered at your school by asking the dean's office or the teacher who is leading the project.

In some cases, service learning will be a part of your schoolwork. You will get credit

toward graduation for the time you put into volunteering. Ask your guidance counselor's or dean's office. Some schools offer credit for volunteering, and others don't. Some schools require that you perform volunteer work to graduate. If this is the case, your guidance counselor will tell you about the school's requirement when you register for classes.

GETTING INVOLVED

Student volunteers usually are the people who develop a school-sponsored project. The teacher who leads the project is there to direct you and your fellow volunteers.

Look around the school or the neighborhood and make a list of things that need improvement. Look for the amount of litter that is inside and outside the school. Do students use plastic folders and notebooks? Check out a local factory for possible pollution abuses.

When a list from each volunteer is presented, take a vote. This vote determines

Working together to help the environment brings people together.

which project the group will develop. This is what happened at Rutledge High School in Rutledge, Tennessee.

Solid-Waste Education

In 1992, a group of students at Rutledge High School in Tennessee noticed the ways in which garbage was being created and disposed of. This is called solid-waste man-agement. They had learned about solid-waste management in the Future Homemakers of America (FHA) club at school. They saw that the school and the community could adopt a better solid-waste management program. With help from their teacher, they planned a solid-waste education program.

Students created flyers and booklets that had information about recycling and litter prevention. They posted the flyers at local businesses and schools. They helped to design billboards with slogans such as "Earth Day Every Day." The students also took a hands-on approach. They adopted a section of a local highway. They clean it several times each year.

PUBLIC AND PRIVATE SPONSORS

Many local and national organizations sponsor service-learning activities. For environmental projects, you can check with groups or clubs that are involved in outdoor activities. These include the Boy Scouts or Girl Scouts, Boys and Girls Clubs of America, and the National 4-H Council.

Congress established the Corporation for National Service in 1993. Its Learn & Serve

Solid waste can be cut down by starting community recycling projects.

America program supports service-learning programs in schools, colleges, and community organizations. (See the resources section for more information.)

Battery Brigade

In Seminole and Volusia counties, Florida, a group of teens developed a recycling program as part of a 4-H project. They called themselves the "Battery Brigade." They contacted the 4-H leaders about how to educate their community in the importance of proper recycling and disposal of batteries. The 4-H leaders helped the students with money needed to print flyers and a special calendar. The leaders also helped the students to organize an educational program. They arranged for booths at fairs and other community events at which they distributed information about battery disposal and recycling. The Battery Brigade even had a special educational program for young children, who use batteries in toys and games.

Government organizations, such as 4-H clubs, are involved with service-learning projects.

FINDING A PROJECT

Finding a project for which to volunteer is easy. All you need to know is whom to ask about volunteering for projects. To find a project at school, ask the sponsoring teacher. That person's name can be found in student bulletins or the student newspaper. Also, contact the dean's office for a list of volunteer projects.

To work with public or private organizations, contact the person who is in charge of their volunteer programs. The National 4-H

Council has an Environmental Stewardship Program. Also, Learn & Serve America and the National Youth Leadership Council sponsor programs nationwide.

Some private organizations may require you to join their organization to volunteer. Call and ask for their youth volunteer coordinator. Girl Scouts of the U.S.A. has environmental activities for Girl Scouts age five to seventeen. Boy Scouts of America offers conservation programs about the use of natural resources. Both organizations work with communities on local, state, or federal environmental projects.

BECOMING A VOLUNTEER

Here are some questions and considerations to think about before volunteering to help with an environmental project:

- Interests. What do you enjoy doing? What type of environmental project would most interest you? If you use neighborhood parks often, helping to clean up a

Girl Scouts earn merit badges by volunteering for environmental projects.

park benefits you and the community. If you like to fish or hike, helping to clean a streambed or repair a trail helps you and others who enjoy the same activity.

- Abilities. What are your skills and talents? Maybe you like to write letters, or work outdoors. Maybe you know a lot about recycling. Each of these skills is needed for different environmental projects. Letters need to be written to environmental agencies and political groups. People are needed to help with outdoor cleanup projects. Your knowledge of recycling can be used at an environmental fair.

- Goals. What are your personal, academic, and career goals? If you start an environmental club, you could educate people in your community about a dangerous area garbage dump, or polluted streams. Running or being a part of this club will help you to focus on your future. Having volunteer experience helps when you

Working as a team to finish a project is part of service-learning success.

apply for college or for work. Choose an activity that will help you to gain the skills needed for a successful future.

• Commitment. How much time can you devote to volunteering for an environmental project? Your schoolwork or after-school job might limit your ability to volunteer for after-school projects. However, you can volunteer with an Adopt-a-Highway program that meets on the weekends. Once you sign up to volunteer on a project, it is important that you be there to work. The project leader and the other volunteers are counting on you!

CHAPTER THREE

PLANNING AN ENVIRONMENTAL PROJECT

So, you have chosen a project and want to plan it yourself. Planning a project on your own is not so difficult a task. If you have volunteered before, then you already know something about how a project is organized. If you are just starting out, the following steps will help you to organize your own project and team.

FORMING A TEAM

You can ask friends, neighbors, schoolmates, and family to be a part of your team. But to find people for a larger group, you will need to print flyers that can be posted around town, at your school, or at your community center. You can create an effective flyer using

Volunteers help everyone with their work in neighborhoods.

a simple word processing program on a computer at home or at school.

Choose people who are interested in the project that you have chosen. If the project requires people to be outdoors, make sure your team knows before the day of the project.

Ask people of all ages to help on the project. Younger kids can do smaller jobs and college students may want to help as well. Finally, choose people who will stay with the project until its completion. Often, only 60 percent of the volunteers actually show up.

FINDING A SPONSOR

Sponsors provide money, time, and other resources for your environmental project. You can ask a parent, teacher, neighbor, or scout leader to sponsor your project. You can also ask your school, or an organization. Call the principal's office at school, or call the youth council of the organization you want to sponsor your project. Tell them what you

Finding a sponsor can help a project with needed money and other important resources.

plan to do, how you plan to do it, and how long it will take.

Your project might require money or supplies, such as markers and poster board, to make posters. Maybe a camera and film are needed to take pictures of a polluted lake. Photos sent with a letter explaining the problem to the Environmental Protection Agency can help to get the lake cleaned.

MAKING A PLAN

Your team must meet to discuss and plan your project. You must decide where—and how often—to meet. Will you need transportation? You may have to ask a parent or a friend to drive you to the meetings.

When you first meet, define your goal for the project. What does your team hope to achieve with its environmental project? Can you achieve all of these goals? If not, how much can you do? Defining your goal may be as simple as writing a paragraph on a piece of paper. For example, let's say you want to clean a vacant lot and make it into a baseball or soccer field. You might write:

"We're going to clear the vacant lot on Elm Street so that we have a place to play soccer. The recyclable trash and nonrecyclable trash will be put in proper bins for the sanitation department to pick up. We will mow the weeds and rake the uneven ground.

Volunteer groups must meet to make a plan for their project.

With help from our sponsor, we will buy grass seed and seed the lot. We will rope off the vacant lot so that the grass will grow. We will post signs so that people know to stay off the lot while the grass grows."

Then, you must decide what each person's job will be. You might need to advertise for more people. Do you have money to print flyers? You might have to take a collection from team members or ask your sponsor for the money.

Next, you must set a schedule. Determine how long the project will take to complete. This depends on what you are trying to achieve and how many people are working with you. By what date do you want the project to be completed?

If completing your project requires money, figure out how much everything will cost. Make a list of what you will need. Will you need equipment (shovels, hammers,

Volunteer projects don't have to be large to help the community.

nails, rakes, etc.)? How about materials (wooden posts, poster board, paper, pens, pencils)? What supplies will your team require (food, water)? If your project is a letter campaign, will you need money for photocopying? How about postage? You can give an estimate of what your project will cost to your sponsor. The sponsor may be able to give you the full amount. If not, you may have to raise funds (see p. 38).

GETTING PERMISSION TO HELP
Helping people or the community may require someone's permission. You might need permission from your school, parents, neighbors, or community organization. If you need the use of a facility, you will have to ask the owners' permission. For example, maybe your school has computers that you need to use to create a petition. Ask a teacher—or the principal—if your group can use them.

Knowing the needs of your project will help it to succeed.

ADVERTISE

Advertising lets the community know what you are doing for the environment. You can advertise if you need more people for your project. Print flyers that call for volunteers. You might be trying to educate the community by holding an environmental fair. Try posting a one-page flyer at school and throughout the community (in shop windows or on light poles).

FUNDRAISING

Sometimes supplies, materials, and equipment can be donated, but other times they

One way to get the word to the community is by creating a press release. This is a written statement that is sent to radio and television stations and newspapers. Here's how to create one:

- Give it a headline ("TEENS FOR RECYCLING")
- Tell your audience who will be involved, what will happen, and when it will happen
- Include the name and telephone number of a contact person

Advertising your project can be as simple as buying poster board and markers to create a sign.

need to be bought. Sponsors can help by donating money. You might get people to donate money through advertising. Or, you could fundraise.

To raise funds, you can shovel snow, mow lawns, rake leaves, wash cars, or paint fences. You also can collect cans, bottles, newspapers, and other recyclable items. Take these to your local recycling center and collect money for your project expenses.

Another way to raise funds is to sell something. You can (with your parents' permission!)

hold a garage sale by collecting unwanted toys, clothes, shoes, etc.

EVALUATING A FINISHED PROJECT

At the end of your project, think about what you have accomplished. Discuss your experience with your team. Talk to your family, teachers, friends, and sponsors. What did you learn and accomplish? What were your feelings, fears, and joys before (and after) the project? Would you do it again? Why or why not?

Write about your experience in a journal. This will allow you to explore your thoughts about your service-learning experience. If you joined a project for school credit, your team leader will probably ask you to do this.

You might find out that you liked volunteering to help the environment. Most people do. When you help people, you feel better about yourself. That helps you to succeed in all areas of your life and prepares you for a successful future.

Writing about your project is a good way to evaluate its success.

NEW WORDS

conservation the act of saving natural resources

environment the world around you

litter trash that is carelessly thrown in the environment and that adds to pollution

natural resources materials from the environment, such as air, water, and fuel, that are necessary for human existence

nonrenewable resources materials such as oil and coal that can't be replaced once they are used up

pollution harmful substances in the air, land, or water

recycle to collect used materials to make into new products

Digeronimo, Theresa. *A Student's Guide to Volunteering*. Franklin Lakes, NJ: Career Press, 1995.

Duper, Linda Leeb. *160 Ways to Help the World: Community Service Projects for Young People*. New York: Facts On File, Inc., 1996.

Fiffer, Steve, and Sharon Sloan Fiffer. *50 Ways to Help Your Community: A Handbook for Change*. New York: Doubleday, 1994.

Goodman, Alan. *The Big Help Book: 365 Ways You Can Make a Difference by Volunteering*. New York: Pocket Books, 1994.

Lewis, Barbara A. *The Kid's Guide to Service Projects*. Minneapolis: Free Spirit Publishing Inc., 1995.

ORGANIZATIONS

Boy Scouts of America
National Office
1325 West Walnut Hill Lane
P.O. Box 152079
Irving, TX 75015-2079
(972) 582-2000
Web site: *www.bsa.scouting.org*

**Boys and Girls
  Clubs of America**
1230 West Peachtree Street, NW
Atlanta, GA 30309
(404) 815-5700
Web site: *www.bgca.org*

Girl Scouts of the U.S.A.
National Headquarters
420 Fifth Avenue
New York, NY 10018-2798
(800) GSUSA4U
Web site: *www.girlscouts.org*

National 4-H Council
7100 Connecticut Avenue
Chevy Chase, MD 20815
(301) 961-2800
Web site: *www.fourhcouncil.edu/*

WEB SITES

CARES (Community Activities Resources Environment Service)
http://library.advanced.org/50017/
This site offers information about the benefits of service learning. It also presents ideas for environmental service-learning projects.

Corporation for National Service: Learn & Serve America!
www.cns.gov/learn/index.html
At this site, you'll learn about service-learning programs in schools and community organizations across the country. You also can find out about honors and scholarships for student volunteers.

U.S. EPA Student Center
www.epa.gov/students/
This site is sponsored by the Environmental Protection Agency. It's filled with valuable information about pollution and the environment, which can help you with your service-learning project.

INDEX

INDEX

ABOUT THE AUTHOR

Suzanne J. Murdico is a freelance writer who specializes in educational books.